Made in the USA
Coppell, TX
11 July 2022

79810162R00068